MW00637557

The Visions of Revelation

Printed in Full Color

As Painted By

Alyce Hart

Alvin Jennings, Compiler

ISBN 1-56794-121-4
Catalog No. C-2442

The Visions of Revelation (58) are also available on 35mm slides in full color for projection in classes, church and school auditoriums, etc. Contact the publisher for information (product #I-1517).

Published by Star Bible Publications • P.O. Box 821220 • Ft. Worth, TX 76182 • 1-800-433-7507

Printed in Singapore

FOREWORD

In this book certain factors should be kept in mind as you look at the paintings and read the material with each one. We are told to "keep things" or remember the words of the prophecy of the Book of Revelation. To do this, we must know what it is we must do, and we must remember to do these things. Where a person can see a picture of the word-text while he is reading he will likely remember the thought much longer. Therefore, the paintings of *The Visions of Revelation* provide a method of remembering the entire Book of The Revelation to John.

The commentary is not given in an effort to interpret the Scriptures for the reader. Rather, its purpose is to point out the relationship of the paintings to the passages of Scripture on which they are based. Interpretations in the paintings are often based on descriptions contained in other parts of the Old and New Testaments. Likewise, new-gained meanings and insights in Revelation are used to illuminate words and passages in other parts of the Bible. Each reader is left with an open mind to form his or her own ideas and conclusions.

The inspiration for the paintings in this book is to be found in the first chapter, third verse, of the Book of The Revelation to John:

> Blessed is he that readeth, and they that hear the words of this prophecy, and keep those things which are written therein: for the time is at hand.

As a young person, the visions recorded in the paintings fascinated me, causing me to wonder just how they would look when put on canvas. After some thirty years of painting, I decided to try to paint them. There were many hours of research spent on each picture before brush ever touched canvas. This research study and soul-searching was necessary to achieving my primary goal of painting symbolically, realistically and authentically. A great portion of the Book of Revelation is written in signs and symbols. Since it was a crime (often punishable by death) to be a professed believer in Jesus Christ, adherers to the Christian faith were forced to conceal their outward displays of religious belief by using secret signs and symbols. Thus symbolism — much of which continues in liturgical use today — became the code language of these early Christians. This material was researched at great length prior to the painting of each picture in an attempt to miss none of the hidden meanings when transferred to canvas.

Most of us miss the beauty recorded in the text of the Book of Revelation because this beauty is more often portrayed in vague and unfamiliar terms and we fail to take the time and the initiative to find their meanings. All of the colors used in the paintings are to be found in the Scripture and in Nature. For example, the fundamental laws of Nature dictate that trees and grass are various tones of green; sky and water are blue; blood is red; and fire is composed of red and yellow hues. Metallic gold is a rich yellow.

The Book of Revelation is written to the angels of the seven Churches in Asia Minor and if the individual church is made up of Christians, the Book is written to Christians.

> I Jesus have sent mine angels to testify unto you these things in the churches. I am the root and the offspring of David, and the bright and morning-star (Rev. 22:16).

There is not a color on the palette that can adequately portray the grandeur of the word-pictures of the scenes described in this Book, or the horror that awaits the sinful; only in the mind can the imagination paint such beauties.

For the Scriptural text of this book, the Book of Revelation is taken from the New International Version of the Holy Bible.*

The commentary or "rationale" used in painting the visions appears at the bottom of each page.

---

* The comments by the author were originally written in 1960 and were based upon the King James Version of 1611. For ease of reading, the NIV text is used in this book but Mrs. Hart's comments are left just as she wrote them. This will account for some variations in wording between the NIV Bible text and her comments.

About The Artist And Her Work . . . .

ALYCE HART

Mrs. Alyce M. Hart lived in Lamesa, Texas, where she was a careful student of her Bible. She attended the Downtown Church of Christ where she was a member. The paintings at first were not done with the intention of having them published, or with the intent of going beyond the realm of family and friends. As the project developed from 1955 to 1960, many individuals and groups asked to see the paintings and hear Mrs. Hart's "commentary" . . . her reasons for the paintings being done as they were. These comments were printed in a small booklet in 1960 in Lubbock, Texas.

At first Mrs. Hart took the original paintings for display to church organizations and study groups, then she began to meet the requests by furnishing colored slides at cost to her ever-widening audience. Star Bible Publications began offering the slides in their catalogs in 1976.

With the publication of the book the painted reproductions appeared with the biblical text (King James Version) on which each picture was based, along with Mrs. Hart's explanation of her approach to the painting.

The book is not a biblical commentary or a concordance. It does not present the viewpoint of any particular church or denomination. Most of the original oil paintings were sold at various auctions, flea markets, etc., and today no complete set exists. The largest collection (about 25) is in the hands of Lubbock Christian University, and a few single originals are held as treasures by special friends.

Mrs. Hart passed from this life on August 10, 1982. It was her intention to print these visions in full color in a book in the early 1960's soon after the work was completed, but it has taken over thirty-five years for her dream to become a reality . . . too late for her to see.

Alvin Jennings,
Publisher

August, 1996

ACKNOWLEDGMENTS

My thanks go to every one that gave encouragement through the five years of planning and painting these pictures. It is wonderful to have people who believe in your ability and tell you so. May you receive a richer and better understanding of others as I have, and make lasting friends that otherwise would have been missed.

Thanks to the school children who came by on their way home from school to watch me paint and give their innocent criticism. I could always count on them to tell the truth about the different objects portrayed.

Thanks also go to the ones who were critical and sometimes even discouraging. Had it not been for them, I might have let down, but they kept me on my toes, causing a greater determination to continue, to be exact, and to give the best of my ability to the work that I was doing. To everyone, may you have this same reaction to do your best when you find others so willing to discourage. Rise above that!

Thanks to those who have offered constructive suggestions, as this is one of the many ways we have of learning.

We, as a family, have gained an abundance of knowledge we would otherwise have missed, had these pictures not been painted. Therefore, it is our wish to share all these things we have learned through reference and research with you, the reader.

The Artist,
Mrs. Alyce Hart

“Blessed Is He That Reads”

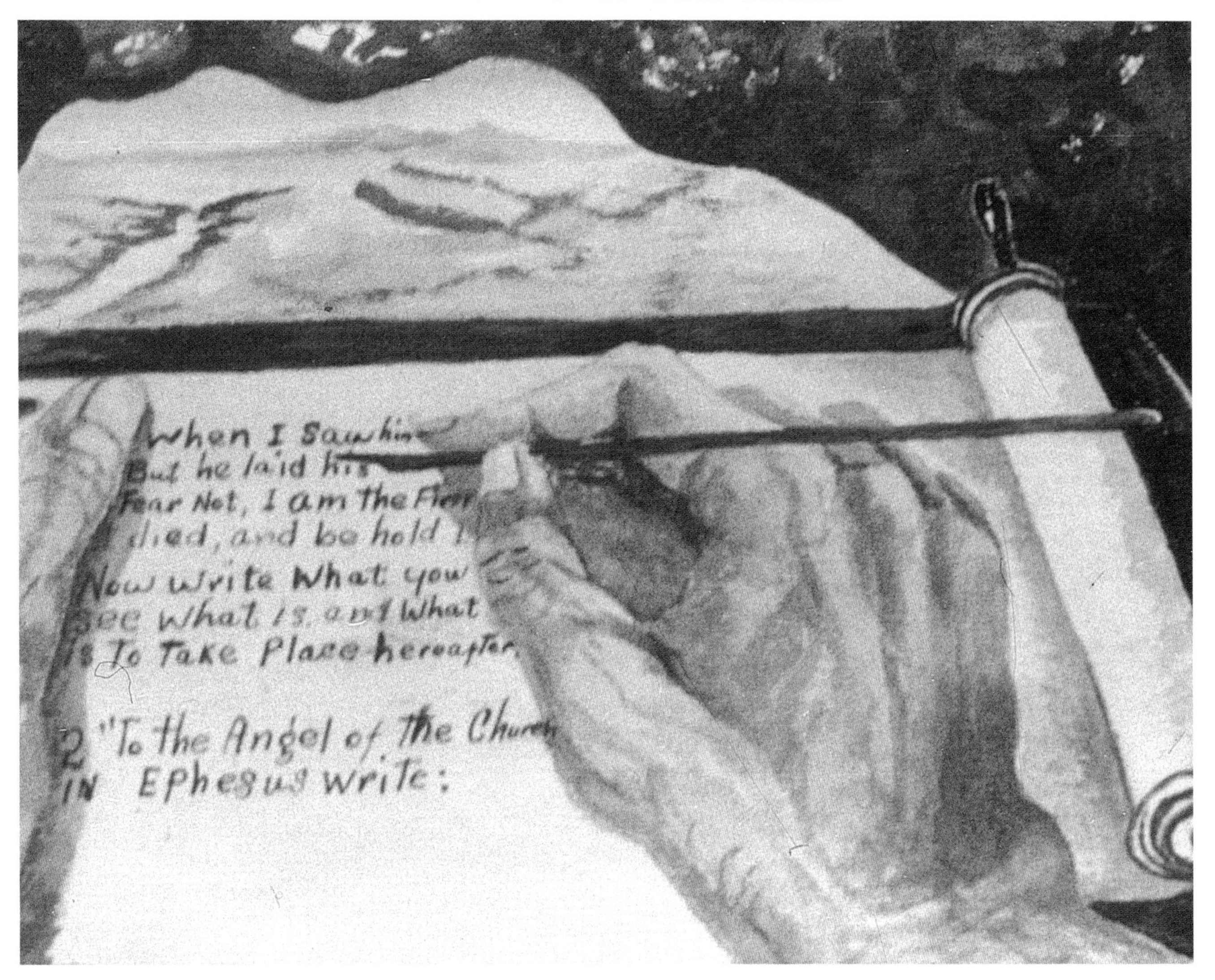

Revelation 1:3

Dear friends, although I was very eager to write to you about the salvation we share, I felt I had to write and urge you to contend for the faith that was once for all entrusted to the saints.

The Isle of Patmos

Revelation 2:12-17
To the Church at Pergamum
[12]"To the angel of the church in Pergamum write:

These are the words of him who has the sharp, double-edged sword. [13]I know where you live—where Satan has his throne. Yet you remain true to my name. You did not renounce your faith in me, even in the days of Antipas, my faithful witness, who was put to death in your city—where Satan live.

[14]Nevertheless, I have a few things against you: You have people there who hold to the teaching of Balaam, who taught Balak to entice the Israelites to sin by eating food sacrificed to idols and by committing sexual immorality. [15]like-wise you also have those who hold to the teaching of Nicolaitans. [16]Repent therefore! Otherwise, I will soon come to you and will fight against them with the sword of my mouth.

[17]He who has an ear, let him hear what the Spirit says to the churches. To him who overcomes, I will give some of the hidden manna. I will also give him a white stone with a new name written on it, known only to him who receives it.

One can gain a better appreciation for the book of Revelation by knowing something of the Isle of Patmos, the place where John was exiled when he saw the visions. Patmos is a very rocky, rugged, bare island in the Aegean Sea, located twenty miles south of Samos and twenty-four miles west of Asia Minor. It is about ten miles long and six miles wide, and is divided into two nearly equal parts by a narrow Isthmus. On the East is the harbor and present town. It is generally thought that John was exiled about 95 A.D. during the reign of Domitian. At that time, offenders were often banished to work in zinc and marble quarries, while some were exiled in loneliness on an island. Most of the information concerning Patmos must come from secular works, as the Scriptures mention it only in Revelation.

Whom Jesus Loved

Revelation 1:1-11

[1]The revelation of Jesus Christ, which God gave him to show his servants what must soon take place. He made it known by sending his angel to his servant John, [2]who testifies to everything he saw—that is, the word of God and the testimony of Jesus Christ. [3]Blessed is the one who reads the words of this prophecy, and blessed are those who hear it and take to heart what is written in it, because the time is near.

[4]John, To the seven churches in the province of Asia: Grace and peace to you from him who is and who was, and who is to come, and from the seven spirits before his throne, [5]and from Jesus Christ, who is the faithful witness, the firstborn from the dead, and the ruler of the kings of the earth.

To him who loves us and has freed us from our sins by his blood, [6]and has made us to be a kingdom and priests to serve his God and Father—to him be glory and power for ever and ever! Amen.

[7]Look, he is coming with the clouds, and every eye will see him, even those who pierced him; and all the peoples of the earth will mourn because of him. So shall it be! Amen.

[8]"I am the Alpha and the Omega," says the Lord God, "who is, and who was, and who is to come, the Almighty."

[9]I, John, your brother and companion in the suffering and kingdom and patent endurance that are ours in Jesus, was on the island of Patmos because of the word of God and the testimony of Jesus. [10]On the Lord's Day I was in the Spirit, and I heard behind me a loud voice like a trumpet, [11]which said: "Write on a scroll what you see and send it to the seven churches: to Ephesus, Smyrna, Pergamum, Thyatira, Sardis, Philadelphia and Laodicea."

The John "whom Jesus loved" was the one chosen to see and write the marvelous things contained in Revelation. He is the last of the apostles mentioned in the Bible. This John, one of the first disciples, was the son of Zebedee and the brother of James. He was a native of Bethsaida in Galilee and a fisherman by occupation. This "Son of Thunder" was a constant companion of Jesus. He went with Him into the death chamber of Jairus' daughter, he saw the glory of the transfiguration, and he was one of the inner three in the garden of Gethsemane. He followed Jesus to the crucifixion, and had committed to his care and keeping the mother of the Lord. He was one of the first to hear of the resurrection, and one of the first to recognize, in the dim haze of the early morning, the presence of the risen Christ. He was with the other apostles when the great commission was given, and was present at the ascension. About sixty years later John was specially blessed again when he was exiled to Patmos and recorded the things which God caused to flit across his enrapt vision. The Bible does not tell of his death.

Like The Son Of Man

Revelation 1:12-20

[12]I turned around to see the voice that was speaking to me. And when I turned I saw seven golden lampstands, [13]and among the lampstands was someone "like a son of man," dressed in a robe reaching down to his feet and with a golden sash around his chest. [14]His head and hair were white like wool, as white as snow, and his eyes were like blazing fire. [15]His feet were like bronze glowing in a furnace, and his voice was like the sound of rushing waters. [16]In his right hand he held seven stars, and out of his mouth came a sharp double-edged sword. His face was like the sun shining in all its brilliance.

[17]When I saw him, I fell at his feet as though dead. Then he placed his right hand on me and said: "Do not be afraid. I am the First and the Last. [18]I am the Living One; I was dead, and behold I am alive for ever and ever! And I hold the keys of death and Hades.

[19]"Write, therefore, what you have seen, what is now and what will take place later. [20]The mystery of the seven stars that you saw in my right hand and of the seven golden lampstands is this: The seven stars are the angels of the seven churches, and the seven lampstands are the seven churches.

There appeared unto John one "like unto the Son of Man." A likeness of Jesus was used to portray the figure. He is dressed in white ("some will walk with me in white") in the mode of dress used 2000 years ago. His girdle is of the type which crossed about the breast. His hair is white "like wool, as white as snow." The eyes were planted with reds and yellows because they were "like flames of fire." The feet being like burnished brass," were painted red, the color of metal when exposed to intense heat. The vision was speaking, hence was painted with mouth slightly open. The stars in His right hand are shown as the heavenly constellations. The brightness of His face is shown by a halo. The two edged sword (their most powerful weapon of offense) is shown proceeding from his mouth. The candlestick was painted according to the description found in Exodus, and is of the type used in worship under the law of Moses.

The sky, clouds and earth were painted so as to show the setting, and the contrast between the spiritual and the human. The prone figure in the blue shows the smallness of man, and his fear and awe at seeing this conquered death, and his experience in witnessing the resurrected Christ. Jesus said, "Fear not ... write the things which thou has seen, and the things which shall be hereafter."

The Church At Ephesus

Revelation 2:1-7

[1] "To the angel of the church in Ephesus write:

These are the words of him who holds the seven stars in his right hand and walks among the seven golden lampstands: [2]I know your deeds, your hard work and your perseverance. I know that you cannot tolerate wicked men, that you have tested those who claim to be apostles but are not, and have found them false. [3]You have persevered and have endured hardships for my name, and have not grown weary.

[4]Yet I hold this against you: You have forsaken your first love. [5]Remember the height from which you have fallen! Repent and do the things you did at first. If you do not repent, I will come to you and remove your lampstand from it's place. [6]But you have this in your favor: You hate the practices of the Nicolaitans, which I also hate.

[7]He who has an ear, let him hear what the Spirit says to the churches. To him who overcomes, I will give the right to eat from the tree of live, which is in the paradise of God.

The background of the cities will play a prominent part in one's understanding of the letters. The pictures are representative of the ruins of the cities many years after John's vision. The brief comments are taken from Smith's Bible Dictionary, 1884 Edition. "EPHESUS, the capital of the roman province of Asia, and an illustrious city in the district of Ionia, nearly opposite the island of Samos. Conspicuous at the head of the harbor of Ephesus was the great temple of Diana ... this building was raised on immense substructions, in consequence of the swampy nature of the ground. The earlier temple, which had been begun before the Persian War, was burnt down in the night when Alexander the Great was born; and another superstructure, raised by the enthusiastic cooperation of all the inhabitants of Asia, had taken its place. The magnificence of this sanctuary was a proverb through the civilized world ... the theater, into which the mob who had seized on Paul, Acts 19:29, rushed was capable of holding 25,000 or 30,000 persons, and was the largest ever built by the Greeks. The stadium or circus, 685 feet long by 200 wide, where the Ephesians held their shows, is probably referred to by Paul as the place where he 'fought with the beasts at Ephesus.' ... The whole place is now utterly desolate, with the exception of the small Turkish village of Ayasaluk. The ruins are of vast extent."

To The Church At Smyrna

Revelation 2:8-11

[8] To the angel of the church in Smyrna write:

These are the words of him who is the First and the Last, who died and came to life again. [9] I know your afflictions and your poverty—yet you are rich! I know the slander of those who say they are Jews and are not, but are a synagogue of Satan. [10] Do not be afraid of what you are about to suffer. I tell you, the devil will put some of you in prison to test you, and you will suffer persecution for ten days. Be faithful, even to the point of death, and I will give you the crown of life.

[11] He who has an ear, let him hear what the Spirit says to the churches. He who overcomes will not be hurt at all by the second death.

"A city of Asia Minor, situated on the Aegean Sea, 40 miles north of Ephesus. It was founded by Alexander the Great and was situated twenty stades (2½ miles) from the city of the same name, which, after a long series of wars with the Lydians, had been finally taken and sacked by Halyattes. The ancient city was built by some piratical Greeks 1500 years before Christ. It seems not impossible that the message to the church in Smyrna contains allusions to the ritual of the pagan mysteries which prevailed in that city. In the time of Strabo, the ruins of the old Smyrna still existed and were partially inhabited, but the new city was one of the most beautiful in all Asia. The streets were laid out as near as might be at right angles. There was a large public library there, and also a handsome building surrounded with porticos which served as a museum. It was consecrated as a heroum to Homer, whom the Smyrnaeans claimed as a countryman. Olympian games were celebrated here, and excited great interest. (Smyrna is still a large city of 180,000 to 200,000 inhabitants, of which a larger proportion are Franks than in any other town in Turkey; 20,000 are Greeks, 9,000 Jews, 8,000 Armenians, 1,000 Europeans, and the rest are Moslems.)"

To The Church At Pergamos

Revelation 2:12-17

[12] "To the angel of the church in Pergamum write:

These are the words of him who has the sharp, double-edged sword. [13] I know where you live—where Satan has his throne. Yet you remain true to my name. You did not renounce your faith in me, even in the days of Antipas, my faithful witness, who was put to death in your city — where Satan lives.

[14] Nevertheless, I have a few things against you: You have people there who hold to the teaching of Balaam, who taught Balak to entice the Israelites to sin by eating food sacrificed to idols and by committing sexual immorality. [15] Likewise you also have those who hold to the teaching of the Nicolaitans. [16] Repent therefore! Otherwise, I will soon come to you and will fight against them with the sword of my mouth.

[17] He who has an ear, let him hear what the Spirit says to the churches. To him who overcomes, I will give some of the hidden manna. I will also give him a white stone with a new name written on it, known only to him who receives it."

"PERGAMOS. A city of Mysia, about 3 miles to the north of the river Caicus, and 20 miles from its present mouth. It was the residence of a dynasty of Greek princes founded after the time of Alexander the Great, and usually called the Attalic dynasty, from its founder, Attalus. The sumptuousness of the Attalic princes had raised Pergamos to the rank of the first city in Asia as regards splendor. The city was noted for its vast library, containing 200,000 volumes. Here was the splendid temples of Zeus or Jupiter, Athene, Apollo and Aesculapius. One of the "seven churches of Asia" was in Pergamos (Rev. 1:1; 2:12-17). It is called "Satan's seat" by John, which some suppose to refer to the worship of Aesculapius, from the serpent being his characteristic emblem. Others refer it to the persecutions of Christians which was the work of Satan. The modern name of the city is Bergama." (*Smith's Bible Dictionary* — article, Pergamos)

To The Church At Thyatira

Revelation 2:18-29

[18] "To the angel of the church in Thyatira write: These are the words of the Son of God, whose eyes are like blazing fire and whose feet are like burnished bronze. [19] I know your deeds, your love and faith, your service and perseverance, and that you are now doing more than you did at first.

[20] Nevertheseess, I have this against you: You tolerate that woman Jezebel, who calls herself a prophetess. By her teaching she misleads my servants into sexual immorality and the eating of food sacrificed to idols. [21] I have given her time to repent of her immorality, but she is unwilling. [22]SoI will cast her on a bed of suffering, and I will make those who commit adultery with her suffer intensely, un-less they repent of her ways. [23] I will strike her children dead. Then all the churches will know that I am he who searches hearts and minds, and I will repay each of you according to your deeds. [24] Now I say to the restr of you in Thyatira, to you who do not hold to her teaching and have not learned Satan's so-called deep secrets (I will not impose any other burden on you): [25] Only hold on to what you have until I come.

[26] To him who overcomes and does my will to the end, I will give authority over the nations —
[27] 'He will rule them with an iron scepter; he will dash them to pieces like pottery' — just as I have received authority from my Father. [28] I will also give him the moring star. [29] He who has an ear, let him hear what the Spirit says to the churches.

"THYATIRA. A city on the Ly-cus, founded by Seleucus Nicator, lay to the left of the road from Pergamos to Sardis, 27 miles from the latter city, and on the very confines of Mysia and Ionia, so as to be some-times reckoned within the one and sometimes within the other. Dyeing apparently formed an important part of the industrial activity of Thyatira, as it did of that of Colossae and Laodicea. It is first mentioned in connection with Lydia, "a seller of purple" (Acts 16:14). One of the Seven Churches of Asia was established here (Rev. 2:18-19). The principal deity of the city was Apollo; but there was another superstition, of an extremely curious nature, which seems to have been brought thither by some of the corrup-ted Jews of the dispersed tribes. A fane stood outside the walls dedicated to Sambatha — the name of the sibyl who is sometimes called Chaldaean, sometimes Jewish, sometimes Persian — in the midst of an enclosure des-ignated "the Chaldaeans' court." This seems to lend an illustration to the obscure passage in Rev. 2:20-21, which some interpret of the wife of the bishop. Now there is evidence to show that in Thyatira there was a great amalgamation of races. If the sibyl Sambatha was in reality a Jewess, lending her aid to the amalgamation of different religions, and not discountenanced by the au-thorities of the Judeo-Christian Church at Thyatira, both the censure and its qualification become easy of explana-tion ... The present city ... has a reputation for the manufacture of scarlet cloth. Its present population is 15,000 to 20,000. There are nine mosques."

(*Smith's Bible Dictionary* — article, Thyatira)

To The Church At Sardis

Revelation 3:1-6

[1] "To the angel of the church in Sardis write: These are the words of him who holds the seven spirits of God and the seven stars. I know your deeds; you have a reputation of being alive, but you are dead. [2] Wake up! Strengthen what remains and is about to die, for I have not found your deeds complete in the sight of my God. Remember, therefore, what you have received and heard; obey it, and repent. But if you do not wake up I will come like a thief and you will not know at what time I will come to you.

[4] Yet you have a few people in Sardis who have not soiled their clothes. They will walk with me, dressed in white, for they are worthy. [5] He who overcomes will, like them, be dressed in white. I will never blot out his name from the book of life, but will acknowledge his name before my Father and his angels. [6] He who has an ear, let him hear what the Spirit says to the churches.

"SARDIS. A city of Asia Minor, and capital of Lydia, situated about two miles to the south of the river Hermus, just below the range of Tmolus, on a spur of which its acropolis was built. It was 50 miles northeast of Smyrna. It was the ancient residence of the kings of Lydia, among them Croesus, proverbial for his immense wealth. Cyrus is said to have taken $600,000,000 worth of treasure from the city when he captured it, B.C. 528. Sardis was, in very early times, both from the extremely fertile character of the neighboring region and from its convenient position, a commercial mart of importance. The art of dyeing wool is said to have been invented here. In the year 214 B.C., it was taken and sacked by the army of Antiochus the Great. Afterward, it passed under the dominion of the kings of Pergamos. Its productive soil must always have continued a source of wealth; but its importance as a central mart appears to have diminished from the time of the invasion of Asia by Alexander. The massive temple of Cybele still bears witness in its fragmentary remains to the wealth and architectural skill of the people that raised it. On the north side of the acropolis, overlooking the valley of the Hermus, is a theater near 400 feet in diameter, attached to a stadium of about 1,000. There are still considerable remains of the ancient city at Sett-Kalessi. Travellers describe the appearance of the locality as that of complete solitude. The only passage in which it is mentioned in the Bible is Rev. 3:1-6."

(*Smith's Bible Dictionary* — article, Sardis).

To The Church At Philadelphia

Revelation 3:7-13

[7] "To the angel of the church in Philadelphia write:

These are the words of him who is holy and true, who holds the key of David. What he opens no one can shut, and what he shuts no one can open. [8] I know your deeds. See, I have placed before you an open door that no one can shut. I know that you have little strength, yet you have kept my word and have not denied my name. [9] I will make those who are of the synagogue of Satan, who claim to be Jews though they are not, but are liars — I will make them come and fall down at your feet and acknowledge that I have loved you. [10] Since you have kept my command to endure patiently, I will also keep you from the hour of trial that is going to come upon the whole world to test those who live on the earth.

[11] I am coming soon. Hold on to what you have so that no one will take your crown. [12] Him who overcomes I will make a pillar in the temple of my God. Never again will he leave it. I will write on him the name of my God and the name of the city of my God, the new Jerusalem, which is coming down out of heaven from my God; and I will also write on him my new name. [13] He who has an ear, let him hear what the Spirit says to the churches.

"PHILADELPHIA (brotherly love), a town on the confines of Lydia and Phrygia Catacecaumene, 25 miles southeast of Sardis, and built by Attalus II, king of Pergamos, who died B.C. 138. It was situated at the lower slopes, and is still represented by a town called Allah-shehr (city of God). Its elevation is 952 feet above the sea. The original population of Philadelphia seems to have been Macedonian; but there was, as appears from Rev. 3:9, a synagogue of Hellenizing Jews there, as well as a Christian church. (It was the seat of one of the 'seven churches of Asia'.) The locality was subject to constant earthquakes, which in the time of Strabo rendered even the town walls of Philadelphia unsafe. The expense of reparation was constant, and hence perhaps the poverty of the members of the church (Rev. 3:8). (The church was highly commended. Rev. 3:7-13). Even Gibbon bears the following well-known testimony to the truth of the prophecy, 'because thou hast kept the word of my patience, I also will keep thee in the hour of temptation': At a distance from the sea, forgotten by the (Greek) emperor, encompassed on all sides by the Turks, her valiant citizens defended their religion and freedom about fourscore years. Among the Greek colonies and churches of Asia, Philadelphia is still erect, a column in a scene of ruins.' 'The modern town, although spacious, containing 3000 houses and 10,000 inhabitants — mostly Turks. A few ruins are found, including remains of a well and about twenty-five churches. In one place are four strong marble pillars, which once supported the dome of a church. One of the old mosques is believed by the native Christians to have been the church in which assembled the primitive Christians addressed in the Apocalypse.' "
(*Smith's Bible Dictionary* — article, Philadelphia).

To The Church At Laodicea

Revelation 3:14-22

[14] To the angel of the church in Laodicea write: These are the words of the Amen, the faithful and true witness, the ruler of God's creation. [15] I know your deeds, that you are neither cold nor hot. I wish you were either one or the other! [16] So, because you are lukewarm — neither hot nor cold — I am about to spit you out of my mouth. [17] You say, 'I am rich; I have acquired wealth and do not need a thing.' But you do not realize that you are wretched, pitiful, poor, blind and naked. [18] I counsel you to buy from me gold refined in the fire, so you can become rich; and white clothes to wear, so you can cover your shameful nakedness; and salve to put on your eyes, so you can see. [19] Those whom I love I rebuke and discipline. So be earnest, and repent. [20] Here I am! I stand at the door and knock. If anyone hears my voice and opens the door, I will come in and eat with him, and he with me. [21] To him who overcomes, I will give the right to sit with me on my throne, just as I overcame and sat down with my Father on his throne. [22] He who has an ear, let him hear what the Spirit says to the churches.

"LAODICEA (justice of the people), a town in the Roman province of Asia, situated in the valley of the Meander, on a small river called the Lycus, with Colossae and Hierapolis a few miles distant to the west. Built, or rather rebuilt, by one of the Seleucie monarchs, and named in honor of his wife, Laodicea became, under the Roman government, a place of some importance. Its trade was consider-able; it lay on the line of a great road; and it was the seat of a conventus. From the third chapter and seventeenth verse of Revelation, we should gather it was a place of great wealth. Christianity was introduced into Laodicea, not however, as it would seem, through the direct agency of Paul. We have good reason for believing that when, in writing from Rome to the Christians of Colossae, he sent a greeting to those of Laodicea, he had not personally visited either place. But the preaching of the gospel at Ephesus, Acts 18:19-19:41, must inevitably have resulted in the formation of churches in the neighboring cities, especially where Jews were settled; and there were Jews in Laodicea. In subsequent times it became a Christian city of eminence, the see of a bishop and a meeting-place of councils. ... Another biblical subject of interest is connected with Laodicea. From Col. 4:16 it appears that St. Paul wrote a letter to this place when he wrote the letter to Colossae. Ussher's view is that it was the same as the Epistle to the Ephesians, which was a circular letter sent to Laodicea among other places. The apocryphal Epistola ad Laodicenses is a late and clumsy forgery." (*Smith's Bible Dictionary* — article, Laodicea).

The Open Door

Revelation 4:1-11

[1]After this I looked, and there before me was a door standing open in heaven. And the voice I had first heard speaking to me like a trumpet said, "Come up here, and I will show you what must take place after this." [2] At once I was in the Spirit, and there before me was a throne in heaven with someone sitting on it. [3]And the one who sat there had the appearance of jasper and carnelian. A rainbow, resembling an emerald encircled the throne. [4] Surrounding the throne were twenty-four other thrones, and seated on them were twenty-four elders. They were dressed in white and had crowns of gold on their heads. [5] From the throne came flashes of lightning, rumblings and peals of thunder. Before the throne, seven lamps were blazing. These are the seven spirits of God. [6] Also before the throne there was what looked like a sea of glass, clear as crystal. In the center, around the throne, were four living creatures, and they were covered with eyes, in front and in back. [7] The first living creature was like a lion, the second was like an ox, the third had a face like a man, the fourth was like a flying eagle. [8] Each of the four living creatures had six wings and was covered with eyes all around, even under his wings. Day and night they never stop saying: "Holy, holy, holy, is the Lord God Almighty, who was, and is, and is to come." [9] Whenever the living creatures give glory, honor and thanks to him wo sits on the throne and who lives for ever and ever, [10] the twenty-four elders fall down before him who sits on the throne, and worship him who lives for ever and ever. They lay their crowns before the throne and say: [11] "You are worthy, our Lord and God, to receive glory and honor and power, for you created all things, and by your will they were created and have their being."

The glory of heavenly worship is the subject of Revelation 4. The splendor and beauty described cannot be grasped by the human mind nor adequately pictured with paint and canvas. The open door is in the clouds because heaven is ordinarily thought of as being above the earth. The great throne, occupied by Him who has all authority, is white. The background is reflected light, signifying that the Light came from the One on the throne. The One who sat upon the throne "was to look upon like a jasper and a sardine stone." The jasper is a milky white stone, while sardius is blood red. Appropriate colors were thus used. The rainbow was "like unto an emerald," hence green received emphasis. The council arrangement with the throne in the center was suggested by the statement, "round about the throne ... I saw four and twenty elders sitting, clothed in white raiment; and they had on their heads crowns of gold." Lightning bolts were used to illustrate thunder. The seven lamps burning before the throne were painted as many lamps ordinarily looked in that day. The floor shows transparency because it was "a sea of glass like unto crystal." This being a heavenly scene, blue was used in the reflections. Much imagination had to be used to paint the four beasts to fit the descriptions given — like unto a lion, ox, man, and eagle — with six wings and full of eyes.

The Scroll And The Lamb

Revelation 5:1-14

[1] Then I saw in the right hand of him who sat on the throne a scroll with writing on both sides and sealed with seven seals.
[2] And I saw a mighty angel proclaiming in a loud voice, "Who is worthy to break the seals and open the scroll?" [3] But no one in heaven or on earth or under the earth could open the scroll or even look inside it. [4] I wept and wept because no one was found who was worthy to open the scroll or look inside. [5] Then one of the elders said to me, "Do not weep! See, the Lion of the tribe of Judah, the Root of David, has triumphed. He is able to open the scroll and its seven seals."
[6] Then I saw a Lamb, looking as if it had been slain, standing in the center of the throne, encircled by the four living creatures and the elders. He had seven horns and seven eyes, which are the seven spirits of God sent out into all the earth. [7] He came and took the scroll from the right hand of him who sat on the throne. [8] And when he had taken it, the four living creatures and the twenty-four elders fell down before the Lamb. Each one had a harp and they were holding golden bowls full of incense, which are the prayers of the saints. [9] And they sang a new song: "You are worthy to take the scroll and open its seals, because you were slain, and with your blood you purchased men for God from every tribe and language and people and nation. [10] You have made them to be a kingdom and priests to serve our God, and they will reign on the earth."
[11] Then I looked and heard the voice of many angels, numbering thousands upon thousands, and ten thousand times ten thousand. They encircled the throne and the living creatures and the elders. [12] In a loud voice they sang: "Worthy is the Lamb, who was slain, to receive power and wealth and wisdom and strength and honor and glory and praise!" [13] Then I heard every creature in heaven and on earth and under the earth and on the sea, and all that is in them, singing: "To him who sits on the throne and to the Lamb be praise and honor and glory and power, for ever and ever!"
[14] The four living creatures said, "Amen," and the elders fell down and worshipped.

This scene is similar to the preceding. A strong angel proclaimed, "Who is worthy to open the book, and to loose the seals thereof?" No man was worthy, but Christ was, and the resultant worship accorded Him is related in the remainder of the chapter. In the picture, John, in blue, may be seen weeping. The Lamb with seven horns and seven eyes is seen with a trickle of blood signifying that He had been slain and that He died for our sins. The scroll in that day was ordinarily a long strip of paper or sheep skins sewed together and rolled on two spools, or on one spool if the scroll was small. Such is painted here, with the Lamb ready to open the seven seals. The twenty-four elders and the four beasts are pictured as they worshipped before the throne, each having a harp and a bowl of incense. The seals were soon to be opened.

The First Seal

Revelation 6:2

[2] I looked, and there before me was a white horse! Its rider held a bow, and he was given a crown, and he rode out as a conqueror bent on conquest.

The seal — always used from Genesis to Revelation as a symbol of authority — was painted in a dull red, the color most commonly used. The scenes in this group are framed with a broken or opened seal so that one can tell at a glance that they are in the same series. The horse, often connected with war and also the fastest form of transportation at that time, was white — a color portraying purity and trust. The horse was painted with a parade prance, showing victory — "conquering and to conquer." The rider carried a bow, a weapon of offense in war. He was given a crown which served to keep his hair from blowing and as a head protector. The precious stones show the rulers and those in authority. The globe of the earth was used to show his destination.

The Second Seal

Revelation 6:3-4

[3] When the Lamb opened the second seal I heard the second living creature say, "Come!" [4] Then another horse came out, a fiery red one. Its rider was given power to take peace from the earth and to make men slay each other. To him was given a large sword.

This horse is pictured as though he were charging into battle. This position was used because the color red was often connected with war and bloodshed, and the rider carried a great sword which was a weapon of offense in war. The sword was one of the earliest weapons known, and one of the most widely used in John's day. It was then used in the fiercest of hand-to-hand combat and seems to have been much shorter and wider than the modern-day sword. The globe of the earth again shows destination.

The Third Seal

Revelation 6:5-6

[5] When the Lamb opened the third seal, I heard the third living creature say, "Come!" I looked, and there before me was a black horse! Its rider was holding a pair of scales in his hand. [6] Then I heard what sounded like a voice among the four living creatures, saying, "A quart of wheat for a day of wages, and three quarts of barley for a day's wages, and do not damage the oil and the wine!"

This horse was painted with a slower gait and more dignified pose because of its color. Black is often connected with mourning and gloom, and pictures that which is dismal and bleak. The rider had a balance — an instrument of weight and measure — in his hand. This was a forerunner of modern scales, and, like modern scales, could mete out just or false weights. The rider was sent to earth.

The Fourth Seal

Revelation 6:7-8

[7] When the Lamb opened the fourth seal, I heard the voice of the fourth living creature say, "Come!" [8] I looked, and there before me was a pale horse! Its rider was named Death, and Hades was following close behind khim. They were given power over a fourth of the earth to kill by sword, famine and plague, and by the wild beasts of the earth.

The color of this horse was "pale", signifying death, and it was painted an ashy white — void of circulation and without life. Its rider's name was Death and is portrayed by a head resembling a skull, with bony hands, arms and feet. Small graves and grave stones can be seen behind the Pale Horse, and following Death. A fourth part of the earth was to suffer death.

The Fifth Seal

Revelation 6:9-11

[9] When he opened the fifth seal, I saw under the altar the souls of those who had been slain because of the word of God and the testimony they had maintained. [10] They called out in a loud voice, "How long, Sovereign Lord, holy and true, until you judge the inhabitants of the earth and avenge our blood?" [11] Then each of them was given a white robe, and they were told to wait a little longer, until the number of their fellow servants and brothers who were to be killed as they had been was completed.

The scene changes from the living to the departed — a place of rest. This seems to be a period of waiting on the part of those who had been slain "for the Word of God, and for the testimony which they held." The altar was designed according to the description given in Exodus of the altar used under the law of Moses. The souls were painted with a human form in a heavenly atmosphere — waiting, milling, resting — wearing white robes which had been given them. They were waiting for a little season until their fellow-servants and brethren should be likewise martyred.

The Sixth Seal

Revelation 6:12-17

[12] I watched as he opened the sixth seal. There was a great earthquake. The sun turned black like sackcloth made of goat hair, the whole moon turned blood red, [13] and the stars in the sky fell to earth, as late figs drop from a fig tree when shaken by a strong wind. [14] The sky receded like a scroll, rolling up, and every mountain and island was removed from its place.

[15] Then the kings of the earth, the princes, the generals, the rich, the mighty, and every slave and every free man hid in caves and among the rocks of the mountains. [16] They called to the mountains and the rocks, "Fall on us and hide us from the face of him who sits on the throne and from the wrath of the Lamb! [17] For the great day of their wrath has come, and who can stand?"

One of the most terrifying scenes in Revelation is pictured here. The wrath of God was described by the fury of the elements. The earth quaked, the sun turned to darkness, the moon as to blood, and the stars fell! The mountains and islands were moved out of their places; and the heaven departed as a scroll! Man was frightened at the thought of facing Him who was sitting on the throne, and he sought to hide in the dens and caves. Crying to the mountains and rocks for a hiding place were people of all classes — kings and slaves, great and small, rich and poor, bond and free.

The scene is still terrifying — WHO SHALL BE ABLE TO STAND?

The Four Winds

Revelation 7:1-8

[1] After this I saw four angels standing at the four corners of the earth, holding back the four winds of the earth to prevent any wind from blowing on the land or on the sea or on any tree. [2] Then I saw another angel coming up from the east, having the seal of the living God. He called out in a loud voice to the four angels who had been given power to harm the land and the sea: [3] "Do not harm the land or the sea or the trees until we put a seal on the foreheads of the servants of our God." [4] Then I heard the number of those who were sealed: 144,000 from all the tribes of Israel. [5] From the tribe of Judah 12,000 were sealed, from the tribe of Reuben 12,000, [6] from the tribe of Asher 12,000, from the tribe of Naphtali 12,000, from the tribe of Manasseh 12,000, [7] from the tribe of Simeon 12,000, from the tribe of Levi 12,000, from the tribe of Issachar 12,000, [8] from the tribe of Zebulun 12,000, from the tribe of Joseph 12,000, from the tribe of Benjamin 12,000.

This scene was difficult to picture. Four angels were standing on the four corners of the earth (a wide expanse to be shown) and holding back four winds (the invisible to be pictured). The figures were composed to be holding back something which could not be seen, but in such a position that one could tell that it was there. John, while watching the scene which to him was future, saw another angel ascend from the east (the rising sun), having the seal of the living God. This angel cried, "Hurt not the earth, neither the sea, nor the trees, till we have sealed the servants of our God in their foreheads." The remaining part of the chapter enumerates the sealing of various ones from the different tribes of Israel.

The Seventh Seal

Revelation 7:9 to 8:5

[9] After this I looked and there before me was a great multitude that no one could count, from every nation, tribe, people and language, standing before the throne and in front of the Lamb. They were wearing white robes and were holding palm branches in their hands. [10] And they cried out in a loud voice: "Salvation belongs to our God, who sits on the throne, and to the Lamb. [11] All the angels were standing around the throne and around the elders and the four living creatures. They fell down on their faces before the throne and worshiped God, [12] saying: "Amen! Praise and glory and wisdom and thanks and honor and power and strength be to our God for ever and ever. Amen!
[13] Then one of the elders asked me, "These in white robes—who are they, and where did they come from?"
[14] I answered, "Sir, you know." And he said, "These are they who have come out of the great tribulation; they have washed their robes and made them white in the blood of the Lamb. [15] Therefore, "they are before the throne of God and serve him day and night in his temple; and he who sits on the throne will spread his tent over them. [16] Never again will they hunger; never again will they thirst. The sun will not beat upon them, nor any scorching heat. [17] For the Lamb at the center of the throne will be their shepherd; he will lead them to springs of living water. And God will wipe away every tear from their eyes."

8 [1] When he opened the seventh seal, there was silence in heaven for about half an hour. [2] And I saw the seven angels who stand before God, and to them were given seven trumpets. [3] Another angel, who had a golden censer, came and stood at the altar. He was given much incense to offer, with the prayers of all the saints, on the golden altar before the throne. [4] The smoke of the incense, together with the prayers of the saints, went up before God from the angel's hand. [5] Then the angel took the censer, filled it with fire from the altar, and hurled it on the earth; and there came peals of thunder, rumblings, flashes of lightning and an earthquake.

This is another overwhelming worship scene. A great multitude — dressed in white robes with palm leaves in their hands — are standing before the throne and the Lamb. An elder inquired of John concerning whether he knew them. Then he said unto John, "These are they which ... have washed their robes, and made them white in the blood of the Lamb." They are here pictured enjoying the beauties of heaven, where they "no more hunger, neither thirst any more; neither shall the sun light them, nor any heat, for the Lamb which is in the midst of the throne shall feed them, and shall lead them unto living fountains of waters; and God shall wipe away all tears from their eyes." What comfort to the faithful!

Silence cannot be painted, but when the seventh seal was opened there was silence for a half-hour. John saw great splendor as the seven angels were given the seven trumpets and as they prepared to sound. Another an-gel, with a golden censer and much incense, came and stood at the golden altar. The altar, censer, and incense were composed according to the description of that used under the law as described in Exodus. Reflections were used to give a heavenly atmosphere.

The First Trumpet

Revelation 8:6-7

[6] Then the seven angels who had the seven trumpets prepared to sound them. [7] The first angel sounded his trumpet, and there came hail and fire mixed with blood, and it was hurled down upon the earth. A third of the earth was burned up, a third of the trees were burned up, and all the green grass was burned up.

The seven angels painted on the cloud at the top left background serve as a guide to show which trumpet is sounding, and they link together the seven trumpets in the same series. At a glance one can tell which trumpet is sounding. One should study the Bible usage of these words: hail, fire, blood, third part, trees, and green grass. The composition uses a forest for the trees and green grass, while storm clouds expel the hail, blood, and fire on the earth. Any one of these would be great destruction, but the combination of the three is used by John to depict the destruction which he saw in this vision.

The Second Trumpet

Revelation 8:8-9

[8] The second angel sounded his trumpet, and something like a huge mountain, all ablaze, was thrown into the sea. A third of the sea turned into blood, [9] a third of the living creatures in the sea died, and a third of the ships were destroyed.

Mountains have often played an important part in the Scriptures — the ark rested on Mount Ararat — the law was given on Mount Sinai — Jesus went to a mountain to pray, and to be tempted, and to teach, and to die, and to ascend. But here is portrayed a terrible scene — an object painted to resemble a mountain on fire, falling into the sea. Shades of reds and yellows show the reflections of fire. One third of the sea turned to blood. Ships, of the type used in that day, were so composed as to show a third part destroyed. Fish were also so painted as to show the number that died. Truly, this is an awful scene of war and bloodshed.

The Third Trumpet

Revelation 8:10-11

[10] The third angel sounded his trumpet, and a great star, blazing like a torch, fell from the sky on a third of the rivers and on the springs of water — [11] the mane of the star is Wormwood. A third of the waters turned bitter, and many people died from the waters that had become bitter.

The star ("burning as it were a lamp") falling from heaven is pictured as it spread out so as to fall on a third of the rivers and on the fountains of waters. The composition of the picture shows a beam of light cast down as the star falling on a third part of the rivers. Rivers, a source of life-sustaining water for man, became bitter and brought death. The star was called "Wormwood", a weed that grew throughout the country, the bitterest thing known at that time. The large river in the center emphasizes the "fountain of waters." On the bank, in left foreground, are small skeletons to portray death. A sickly color of green was chosen to show the bitterness of the water and to conform to the peculiar color of the plant.

The Fourth Trumpet

Revelation 8:12

> [12] The fourth angel sounded his trumpet, and a third of the sun was struck, a third of the moon, and a third of the stars, so that a third of them turned dark. A third of the day was without light, and also a third of the night.

In this vision, both day and night were darkened "a third part." An arc was designed to represent the earth, and the continents shown are the ones which were enlightened at that time, the places where the gospel had been preached and the church established. The remainder of the composition shows converging day and night. The sun, moon, and stars are placed in their proper relationship, and the darkening of the third part of each is shown as it effected the earth.

The Eagle

Revelation 8:13

> [13] As I watched, I heard an eagle that was flying in midair call out in a loud voice: "Woe! Woe! Woe to the inhabitants of the earth, because of the trumpet blasts about to be sounded by the other three angels!"

Between the fourth and fifth trumpets, John heard an eagle (angel — King James Version) crying as it flew in mid-heaven. The Golden eagle was chosen to portray this scene. Its size, fierceness, strength, and speed seems to better fit it for the purpose. It is shown with its beak parted, crying "Woe, Woe, Woe". The color of the feathers, as they catch the rays of light while in motion, have a golden appearance with all its gleaming and shimmering effects.

This seems to be an advance warning of the terrible things to come in the sounding of the last three trumpets.

The Fifth Trumpet

Revelation 9:1-12

[1] The fifth angel sounded his trumpet, and I saw a star that had fallen from the sky to the earth. The star was given the key to the shaft of the Abyss. [2] When he opened the Abyss, smoke rose from it like the smoke from a gigantic furnace. The sun and sky were darkened by the smoke from the Abyss. [3] And out of the smoke locusts came down upon the earth and were given power like that of scorpions of the earth. [4] They were told not to harm the grass of the earth or any plant or tree, but only those people who did not have the seal of God on their foreheads. [5] They were not given power to kill them, but only to torture them for five months. And the agony they suffered was like that of the sting of a scorpion when it strikes a man. [6] During those days men will seek death, but will not find it; they will long to die, but death will elude them.

[7] The locusts looked like horses prepared for battle. On their heads they word something like crowns of gold, and their faces resembled human faces. [8] Their hair was like lions' teeth. [9] They had breastplates like breastplates of iron, and the sound of their wings was like the thundering of many horses and chariots rushing into battle. [10] They had tails and stings like scorpions, and in their tails they had power to torment people for five months. [11] They had as king over them the angel of the Abyss, whose name in Hebrew is Abaddon, and in Greek, Apollyon.

[12] The first woe is past; two other woes are yet to come.

This picture was composed after much research, and the objects designed accordingly. The key (used then as now) is large — as were all keys in that day. The pit — a place of darkness, bitterness, and corruption — is set in a rocky and secluded spot, signifying that it is away from the Truth. Locusts, the destructive type, of the grasshopper family, were told to hurt "only those men who have not the seal of God in their foreheads." They were to torment men, but not to kill them — however, the torment would be so intense as to make death desirable. An effort was made to picture the locusts in full detail — shaped like horses, faces of men, hair of women, teeth like lions, breast-plates of iron, wings in motion, tails like scorpions, and stings in their tails. This is another scene of terror.

The Sixth Trumpet

Revelation 9:13-21

[13] The sixth angel sounded his trumpet, and I heard a voice coming from the horns of the golden altar that is before God. [14] It said to the sixth angel who had the trumpet, "Release the four angels who are bound at the great river Euphrates." [15] And the four angels who had been kept ready for this very hour and day and month and year were released to kill a third of mankind. [16] The number of the mounted troops was two hundred million. I heard their number.

[17] The horses and riders I saw in my vision looked like this: Their breastplates were fiery red, dark blue, and yellow as sulfur. The heads of the horses resembled the heads of lions and out of their mouths came fire, smoke and sulfur. [18] A third of mankind was killed by the three plagues of fire, smoke and sulfur that came out of their mouths. [19] The power of the horses was in their mouths and in their tails; for their tails were like snakes, having heads with which they inflict injury.

[20] The rest of mankind that were not killed by these plagues still did not repent of the work of their hands; they did not stop worshiping demons, and idols of gold, silver, bronze, stone and wood — idols that cannot see or hear or walk. [21] Nor did they repent of their murders, their magic arts, their sexual immorality or their thefts.

The arrangement of this picture shows the river Euphrates and the terrain which surrounds it. The four angels were bound, but to be loosed to command a large cavalry. The horse-men had breastplates of jacinth and brimstone, hence shades of red, bright blue, and yellow were used. John saw the heads of horses were like lions with fire and smoke, and brimstone coming from their mouths. Their tails were like serpents and they had the power to hurt. A third part of men were killed, but the rest of the men continued and refused to repent.

The Strong Angel With The Book

Revelation 10:1-11

[1] Then I saw another mighty angel coming down from heaven. He was robed in a cloud, with a rainbow above his head; his face was like the sun, and his legs were like fiery pillars. [2] He was holding a little scroll, which lay open in his hand. He planted his right foot on the sea and his left foot on the land, [3] and he gave a loud shout like the roar of a lion. When he shouted, the voices of the seven thunders spoke. [4] And when the seven thunders spoke, I was about to write; but I heard a voice from heaven say, "Seal up what the seven thunders have said and do not write it down."

[5] Then the angel I had seen standing on the sea and on the land raised his right hand to heaven. [6] And he swore by him who lives for ever and ever, who created the heavens and all that is in them, the earth and all that is in it, and the sea and all that is in it, and said, "There will be no more delay! [7] But in the days when the seventh angel is about to sound his trumpet, the mystery of God will be accomplished, just as he announced to his servants the prophets."

[8] Then the voice that I had heard from heaven spoke to me once more: "Go, take the scroll that lies open in the hand of the angel who is standing on the sea and on the land."

[9] So I went to the angel and asked him to give me the little scroll. He said to me, "Take it and eat it. It will turn your stomach sour, but in your mouth it will be as sweet as honey."

[10] I took the little scroll from the angels hand and ate it. It tasted as sweet as honey in my mouth, but when I had eaten it, my stomach turned sour. [11] Then I was told, "You must prophesy again about many peoples, nations, languages and kings."

This vision is introduced by a strong angel coming down from heaven, having a rainbow upon his head and his face as bright as the sun, and his feet like pillars of fire. In his hand he had a little book opened. His right foot was on the sea and the left on the earth. He lifted up his hand toward heaven. The figure was given human form with the detail followed very closely. The seven lightning bolts portray the seven thunders which John heard. The cloud was used for clothing, the rainbow for head covering, and the brightness of his face was emphasized. A careful study of this chapter leaves one with a strong admiration for this vision of beauty.

John With A Reed

Revelation 11:1-14

[1] I was given a reed like a measuring rod and was told, "Go and measure the temple of God and the altar, and count the worshipers there. [2] But exclude the outer court; do not measure it, because it has been given to the Gentiles. They will trample on the holy city for 42 months. [3] And I will give power to my two witnesses, and they will prophesy for 1,260 days, clothed in sackcloth." [4] These are the two olive trees and the two lampstands that stand before the Lord of the earth. [5] If anyone tries to harm them, fire comes from their mouths and devours their enemies. This is how anyone who wants to harm them must die. [6] These men have power to shut up the sky so that it will not rain during the time they are prophesying; and they have power to turn the waters into blood and to strike the earth with every kind of plague as often as they want.

[7] Now when they have finished their testimony, the beast that comes up from the Abyss will attack them, and overpower and kill them. [8] Their bodies will lie in the street of the great city, which is figuratively called Sodom and Egypt, where also their Lord was crucified. [9] For three and a half days men from every people, tribe, language and nation will gaze on their bodies and refuse them burial. [10] The inhabitants of the earth will gloat over them and will celebrate by sending each other gifts, because these two prophets had tormented those who live on the earth.

[11] But after the three and a half days a breath of life from God entered them, and they stood on their feet, and terror struck those who saw them. [12] Then they heard a loud voice from heaven saying to them, "Come up here." And they went up to heaven in a cloud, while their enemies looked on.

[13] At that very hour there was a severe earthquake and a tenth of the city collapsed. Seven thousand people were killed in the earth quake, and the survivors were terrified and gave glory to the God of heaven.

[14] The second woe has passed; the third woe is coming soon.

This scene pictures John as he measures the temple, altar, and worshippers. He used a reed — which was a water plant which grows from three to six feet high, and sometimes called a bulrush, or papyrus; the joints were used for measuring rods. The building was composed to resemble a place of worship, with figures and an altar inside. The temple was enclosed with a wall so as to show the outer court. John stands in the doorway. The two witnesses — the two lamp-stands and the two olive trees — can be seen in the center foreground. The olive tree was a source of oil and very essential to sustaining life. The candle-stick was used in worship, and was later a symbol of light.

The Seventh Trumpet

Revelation 11:15-19

[15] The seventh angel sounded his trumpet and there were loud voices in heaven which said: "The kingdom of the world has become the kingdom of our Lord and of his Christ, and he will reign for ever and ever."
[16] And the twenty-four elders, who were seated on their thrones before God, fell on their faces and worship God, [17] saying: "We give thanks to you Lord God Almighty, the One who is and who was, because you have taken your great power and have begun to reign.
[18] The nations were angry; and your wrath has come. The time has come for judging the dead, and for rewarding your servants the prophets and your saints and those who reverence your name, both small and great — and for destroying those who destroy the earth."
[19] Then God's temple in heaven was opened, and within his temple was seen the ark of his covenant. And there came flashes of lightning, rumblings, peals of thunder, an earthquake and a great hailstorm.

In this picture John sees the heavenly scene of rejoicing as the voices sang, "The kingdoms of this world are become the kingdoms of our Lord, and of His Christ: and He shall reign forever and ever." The twenty-four elders sitting in God's presence fell on their faces and worshipped. The ark portrays the temple opened in heaven. And it is said there were, "lightnings, and voices, and thunderings, and an earthquake, and great hail."

The Woman And The Dragon

Revelation 12:1-6

[1] A great and wondrous sign appeared in heaven: a woman clothed with the sun, with the moon under her feet and a crown of twelve stars on her head. [2] She was pregnant and cried out in pain as she was about to give birth. [3] Then another sign appeared in heaven: an enormous red dragon with seven heads and ten horns and seven crowns on his heads. [4] His tail swept a third of the stars out of the sky and flung them to the earth. The dragon stood in front of the woman who was about to give birth, so that he might devour her child the moment it was born. [5] She gave birth to a son, a male child, who will rule all the nations with an iron scepter. And her child was snatched up to God and to his throne. [6] The woman fled into the desert to a place prepared for her by God, where she might be taken care of for 1,260 days.

John here saw a fascinating vision. A woman clothed (draped in the fashion of the day) with the sun, (a sphere painted in reds and yellows) and the moon (another sphere) under her feet, and upon her head a crown of twelve stars; and she being with child crieth (face distorted with pain), travailing in birth, and pained to be delivered. Another wonder appeared in heaven — a great red dragon, with seven heads and seven crowns. His tail swept a third part of the stars from heaven, throwing them down to the earth. He was waiting to devour the unborn child. Inasmuch as the child was born to rule the nations with a rod of iron, the dragon failed in his mission to devour it. The child was caught up unto God, and the woman hid in the wilderness. Good eventually triumphs over evil.

War In Heaven

Revelation 12:7-12

7 And there was war in heaven. Michael and his angels fought against the dragon, and the dragon and his angels fought back. 8 But he was not strong enough, and they lost their place in heaven.
9 The great dragon was hurled down — that ancient serpent called the devil, or Satan, who leads the whole world astray. He was hurled to the earth, and his angels with him.
10 Then I heard a loud voice in heaven say: "Now have come the salvation and the power and the kingdom of our God, and the authority of his Christ. For the accuser of our brothers, who accuses them before our God day and night, has been hurled down.
11 They overcame him by the blood of the Lamb and by the word of their testimony; they did not love their lives so much as to shrink from death.
12 Therefore rejoice, you heavens and you who dwell in them! But woe to the earth and the sea, because the devil has gone down to you! He is filled with fury, because he knows that his time is short."

This setting is in heaven. The dragon had been defeated in his attempt to devour the child (Rev. 12:4-5), and he made war in heaven — but was again defeated. With his angels he was cast out. In this painting, the sky is used as the background, signifying heaven. The clouds show the majestic glory of the heavens. Figures are clad in white, showing purity. They are shown above as the dragon, painted in human form, is cast down, with his angels scattered about him as they fall from heaven.

The Woman With Two Wings

Revelation 12:13-17

13 When the dragon saw that he had been hurled to the earth, he pursued the woman who had given birth to the mail child. 14 The woman was given the two wings of a great eagle, so that she might fly to the place prepared for her in the desert, where she would be taken care of for a time, times and half a time, out of the serpent's reach. 15 Then from his mouth the serpent spewed water like a river, to overtake the woman and sweep her away with the torrent. 16 But the earth helped the woman by opening its mouth and swallowing the river that the dragon had spewed out of his mouth. 17 Then the dragon was enraged at the woman and went off to make war against the rest of her offspring — those who obey God's commandments and hold to the testimony of Jesus.

The scene here changes to earth. The dragon seems to be more and more enraged. In a vain effort to destroy the woman, he casts water, as a flood, out of his mouth, but the earth opens up and swallows the water and the woman was given two great wings that she might escape. The dragon then makes war with her seed, those who keep God's commandments. The picture shows the woman, with wings of an eagle, in flight. The male child is at the throne of God. The devil, in dragon form, with water pouring from the mouths and the earth swallowing the flood, is also pictured. Colors used are from natural laws — sky, shades of blue; grass, green of the proper shade; mountains, in the haze for distance; and the land, in its proper color.

The Seven Headed Beast Of The Sea

Revelation 13:1-10

[1] And the dragon stood on the shore of the sea. And I saw a beast coming out of the sea. He had ten horns and seven heads, with ten crowns on his horns, and on each head a blasphemous name. [2] The beast I saw resembled a leopard, but had feet like those of a bear and a mouth like that of a lion. The dragon gave the beast his power and his throne and great authority. [3] One of the heads of the beast seemed to have had a fatal wound, but the fatal wound had been healed. The whole world was astonished and followed the beast. [4] Men worshiped the dragon because he had given authority to the beast, and they also worshiped the beast and asked, "Who is like the beast? Who can make war against him?"
[5] The beast was given a mouth to utter proud words and blasphemies and to exercise his authority for forty-two months. [6] He opened his mouth to blaspheme God, and to slander his name and his dwelling place and those who live in heaven. [7] He was given power to make war against the saints and to conquer them. And he was given authority over every tribe, people, language and nation. [8] All inhabitants of the earth will worship the beast — all whose names have not been written in the book of life belonging to the Lamb that was slain from the creation of the world.
[9] He who has an ear, let him hear.
[10] If anyone is to go into captivity, into captivity he will go. If anyone is to be killed with the sword, with the sword he will be killed. This calls for patient endurance and faithfulness on the part of the saints.

John stands on the sands of the sea, and sees another menace to the saints. He describes it as a beast having seven heads, ten horns, and ten crowns. Looking closer, it was like a leopard, having feet like a bear, and the mouth of a lion. The dragon gave him power and authority. One of the heads was wounded to death, but healed. This beast had great power, and the backing of the dragon. Many worshipped him. Saints were persecuted, and God was blasphemed. But he could not be ultimate victor over those whose names are in the Lamb's Book of Life.

The figure, with a leopard's spots, a bear's feet, and a lion's mouth, is a composition of the imagination. Combining all the descriptions, a beast is pictured standing on the sea with seven heads and but one body. The lower head is drooping, signifying the wounded one. The colors were taken from natural law, combining the colors of the leopard, bear, and lion.

The False Prophet

Revelation 13:11-18

[11] Then I saw another beast, coming out of the earth. He had two horns like a lamb, but he spoke like a dragon. [12] He exercised all the authority of the first beast on his behalf, and made the earth and its inhabitants worship the first beast, whose fatal wound had been healed. [13] And he performed great and miraculous signs, even causing fire to come down from heaven to earth in full view of men. [14] Because of the signs he was given power to do on behalf of the first beast, he deceived the inhabitants of the earth. He ordered them to set up an image in honor of the beast who was wounded by the sword and yet lived. [15] He was given power to give breath to the image of the first beast, so that it could speak and cause all who refused to worship the image to be killed. [16] He also forced everyone, small and great, rich and poor, free and slave, to receive a mark on his right hand or on his forehead, [17] so that no one could buy or sell unless he had the mark, which is the name of the beast or the number of his name.

[18] This calls for wisdom. If anyone has insight let him calculate the number of the beast, for it is man's number. His number is 666.

John describes another deceptive force — a beast coming up out of the earth. He had two horns, and spoke like a dragon. He did many wonders — like making fire come down from heaven — and thus deceived many into worshipping the beast. He spoke — as through the image of the beast — and led many astray.

The sheep pictured is of the broad-tailed variety of that day. It has two horns, and the mouth and under the neck is painted red, to portray the dragon standing on a higher elevation looking down at an image of the beast. All the people are worshipping it. Fire is seen coming down from heaven to illustrate the great wonders. The beast had a number and those with wisdom could count it — 666.

The Lamb of Mount Sion

Revelation 14:1-13

[1] Then I looked, and there before me was the Lamb, standing on Mount Zion, and with him 144,000 who had his name and his Father's name written on their foreheads. [2] And I heard a sound from heaven like the roar of rushing waters and like a loud peal of thunder. The sound I heard was like that of harpists playing their harps. [3] And they sang a new song before the throne and before the four living creatures and the elders. No one could learn the song except the 144,000 who had been redeemed from the earth.

[4] These are those who did not defile themselves with women, for they kept themselves pure. They follow the Lamb wherever he goes. They were purchased from among men and offered as firstfruits to God and the Lamb. [5] No lie was found in their mouths; they are blameless.

[6] Then I saw another angel flying in midair, and he had the eternal gospel to proclaim to those who live on the earth — to every nation, tribe, language and people. [7] He said in a loud voice, "Fear God and give him glory, because the hour of his judgment has come. Worship him who made the heavens, the earth, the sea and the springs of water."

[8] A second angel followed and said, "Fallen! Fallen is Babylon the Great, which made all the nations drink the maddening wine of her adulteries."

[9] A third angel followed them and said in a loud voice: "If anyone worships the beast and his image and receives his mark on the forehead or on the hand, [10] he, too, will drink of the wine of God's fury, which has been poured full strength into the cup of his wrath. He will be tormented with burning sulfur in the presence of the holy angels and of the Lamb.

[11] And the smoke of their torment rises for ever and ever. There is no rest day or night for those who worship the beast and his image, or for anyone who receives the mark of his name." [12] This calls for patient endurance on the part of the saints who obey God's commandments and remain faithful to Jesus.

[13] Then I heard a voice from heaven say, "Write: Blessed are the dead who die in the Lord from now on." "Yes," says the Spirit, "they will rest from their labor, for their deeds will follow them."

The theme changes. John sees a Lamb on Mount Sion, and recognizes this force — the greatest in heaven and earth. With Him are the 144,000 — the ones redeemed from the earth — having the Father's name written in their foreheads. A pure white sheep was used — and placed on a very high mountain, with the Lamb in front of the figures in white. The letter "G" on their foreheads shows the Father's name.

During the vision, an angel was flying in the midst of heaven, having the everlasting gospel, to preach to "them that dwell on the earth, and to every nation, and kindred, and tongue, and people." Another angel followed pronouncing doom upon Babylon, the city of sin. The third angel followed with a message to the ones who had received the mark of the beast.

The three angels flying in the sky are shown very close to the Lamb and the Redeemed. The background is painted according to the natural colors.

The Son of Man on a White Cloud

Revelation 14:14-16

[14] I looked, and there before me was a white cloud, and seated on the cloud was one "like a son of man" with a crown of gold on his head and a sharp sickle in his hand. [15] Then another angel came out of the temple and called in a loud voice to him who was sitting on the cloud, "Take your sickle and reap, because the time to reap has come, for the harvest of the earth is ripe." [16] So he who was seated on the cloud swung his sickle over the earth, and the earth was harvested.

The setting of this scene is again in the heavens. A figure with the likeness of Jesus glorified is seated on a white cloud, wearing a gold crown (authority) and a sickle (instrument of harvest) in His hand. An angel announced that the harvest was ready. Mankind was ready to turn from evil!

The Two Angels

Revelation 14:17-20

[17] Another angel came out of the temple in heaven, and he too had a sharp sickle. [18] Still another angel, who had charge of the fire, came from the altar and called in a loud voice to him who had the sharp sickle, "Take your sharp sickle and gather the clusters of grapes from the earth's vine, because its grapes are ripe." [19] The angel swung his sickle on the earth, gathered its grapes and threw them into the great winepress of God's wrath. [20] They were trampled in the winepress outside the city, and blood flowed out of the press, rising as high as the horses' bridles for a distance of 1,600 stadia. *(about 180 miles)*

During the harvest of the righteous souls, another angel with a sharp sickle came out of the temple in heaven, and another came from the altar. The harvest scene follows. On a cloud in the upper left background is the angel of the Altar, telling the angel with the sickle what to do. A figure is flying close to the vineyards. The winepress is in the left foreground with a city to the right, signifying that the scene is outside the city. Vineyards are pictured as planted on terraces on the sides of hills and mountains. The landscape which serves as a background shows a valley where the blood is flowing a great distance, and the depth of it is pictured by the horse's head in the center foreground. This ancient type winepress is used even today. Men were stripped to the loin cloth where they held to thongs in the center as they tramped the grapes with their feet.

The Seven Last Plagues

Revelation 15:1-8

[1] I saw in heaven another great and marvelous sign: seven angels with the seven last plagues — last, because with them God's wrath is completed. [2] And I saw what looked like a sea of glass mixed with fire and, standing beside the sea, those who had been victorious over the beast and his image and over the number of his name. They held harps given them by God [3] and sang the song of Moses the servant of God and the song of the Lamb: "Great and marvelous are your deeds, Lord God Almighty. Just and true are your ways, King of the ages. [4] Who will not fear you, O Lord, and bring glory to your name? For you alone are holy. All nations will come and worship you, for your righteous acts have been revealed."
[5] After this I looked and in heaven the temple, that is, the tabernacle of the Testimony, was opened.
[6] Out of the temple came the seven angels with the seven plagues. They were dressed in clean, shinning linen and wore golden sashes around their chests. [7] Then one of the four living creatures gave to the seven angels seven golden bowls filled with the wrath of God, who lives for ever and ever. [8] And the temple was filled with smoke from the glory of God and from his power, and no one could enter the temple until the seven plagues of the seven angels were completed.

Great and marvelous is the heavenly scene which John describes in the fifteenth chapter. Seven angels, with the seven last plagues, were standing on the sea of glass mingled with fire. The victors had their harps, and they sang "the song of Moses the servant of God, and the song of the Lamb, saying, Great and marvelous are Thy works, Lord God Almighty; just and true are Thy ways, Thou King of the saints."

At this time, the temple of the tabernacle of testimony was opened and the seven angels were seen coming out, having the seven last plagues. They were dressed in pure white linen, and girded about with golden girdles. They carried seven golden vials filled with the wrath of God.

The heavenly tabernacle was painted according to the description of the Tabernacle in Moses' day, given in Exodus. All the proper colors are shown in the painting. At the top background can be seen the pillars of the temple with the smoke from the glory of God. The victors are shown in the right middle background. The seven angels with white robes, golden girdles and holding the seven bowls of wrath are in front of the tabernacle.

The First Bowl of Wrath

Revelation 16:1, 2

[1] Then I heard a loud voice from the temple saying to the seven angels, "Go, pour out the seven bowls of God's wrath on the earth."
[2] The first angel went and poured out his bowl on the land, and ugly and painful sores broke out on the people who had the mark of the beast and worshiped his image.

When the first vial of wrath was poured out upon the earth, a noisome and grievous sore fell upon the men who had the mark of the beast. In the painting, at the top left background, is seen the tabernacle with the seven angels (in white, with golden girdles and golden bowls) on a floating cloud, pouring out the wrath from above. The setting for this scene is a city with many people suffering from the plague of sores. Some are lying down, some sitting, and some are showing extreme pain. This is a most unpleasant scene.

The Second Bowl of Wrath

Revelation 16:3

[3] The second angel poured out his bowl on the sea, and it turned into blood like that of a dead man, and every living thing in the sea died.

When the second bowl was poured out, the sea became as a dead man's blood, and every living soul therein died. The setting of the picture is a sea colored as a "dead man's blood" — a darker color than the bright red which usually pictures blood. It is wavy, suggesting coagulation of blood. Clefts and distant mountains are used to show the sea in its proper setting. Dead fish indicate the result of the plague. The seven angels are seen at the top left background, with the second angel pouring out the contents of his bowl.

The Third Bowl of Wrath

Revelation 16:4-7

[4] The third angel poured out his bowl on the rivers and springs of water, and they became blood. [5] Then I heard the angel in charge of the waters say: "You are just in these judgments, you who are and who were, the Holy One, because you have so judged: [6] for they have shed the blood of your saints and prophets, and you have given them blood to drink as they deserve."

The third angel poured his bowl of wrath on the rivers and fountains of waters, and they became blood. The angels proclaimed the righteousness of God in so judging. The picture shows rivers, painted red, flowing into larger ones, with mountains used for background, and palms showing climatic conditions — and also portraying possible peace.

The Fourth Bowl of Wrath

Revelation 16:8, 9

[8] The fourth angel poured out his bowl on the sun, and the sun was given power to scorch people with fire. [9] They were seared by the intense heat and they cursed the name of God, who had control over these plagues, but they refused to repent and glorify him.

The pouring out of the fourth bowl upon the sun gave him power to scorch men with fire. This plague caused men to blaspheme instead of bringing them to repentance. A desolate and barren background was chosen to show the effect of this heat on men stricken by the fire from the sun. The figure standing, robed in white, had not been overcome. The trees are pictured with fallen leaves with the bare earth stretching out in all directions as far as the eye can see.

The Fifth Bowl of Wrath

Revelation 16:10, 11

[10] The fifth angel poured out his bowl on the throne of the beast, and his kingdom was plunged into darkness. Men gnawed their tongues in agony [11] and cursed the God of heaven because of their pains and their sores, but they refused to repent of what they had done.

The fifth angel poured out his vial upon the seat of the beast. The result was the darkening of his kingdom, and great pain on the part of his followers. Again, instead of repentance, there was blasphemy. The seat, or throne, was elevated, with steps to the top. It was designed with the face of a beast on the front of the arm rests. Buildings were composed so as to show the type of architecture used. Figures, in different positions, show the effect of their affliction with their misery and suffering.

The Sixth Bowl of Wrath

Revelation 16:12-16

[12] The sixth angel poured out his bowl on the great river Euphrates, and its water was dried up to prepare the way for the kings from the east. [13] Then I saw three evil spirits that looked like frogs; they came out of the mouth of the dragon, out of the mouth of the false prophet. [14] They are spirits of demons performing miraculous signs, and they go out to the kings of the whole world, to gather them for the battle on the great day of God Almighty.

[15] "Behold, I come like a thief! Blessed is he who stays awake and keeps his clothes with him, so that he may not go naked and be shamefully exposed."

[16] Then they gathered the kings together to the place that in Hebrew is called Armageddon.

The sixth bowl of wrath was poured out upon the river Euphrates. The waters were dried up (a slow process) to prepare the way for the king of the East. John saw three unclean spirits (as frogs) coming out of the mouths of the dragon, beast, and false prophet. They worked miracles, and went to the king of the earth to gather them to the great battle.

The composition pictures the river Euphrates (the longest and largest in Western Asia) as barren and dry. The frogs, representing the evil spirits, are shown coming from the mouths of the dragon and beast. The picture presents the preparing for the "way of the kings of the east".

The Seventh Bowl of Wrath

Revelation 16:17-21

[17] The seventh angel poured out his bowl into the air, and out of the temple came a loud voice from the throne, saying, "It is done!" [18] Then there came flashes of lightning, rumblings, peals of thunder and a severe earthquake. No earthquake like it has ever occurred since man has been on earth, so tremendous was the quake. [19] The great city split into three parts, and the cities of the nations collapsed. God remembered Babylon the Great and gave her the cup filled with the wine of the fury of his wrath. [20] Every island fled away and the mountains could not be found. [21] From the sky huge hailstones of about a hundred pounds each fell upon men. And they cursed God on account of the plague of hail, because the plague was so terrible.

When the seventh bowl was poured out into the air, a great disturbance followed — thunders, lightnings, an earthquake so great that cities fell, islands fled away and mountains were not found. The great city "was divided into three parts" and Babylon "came in remembrance before God." A great hail, every stone a hundred weight, fell on men. Man continued to blaspheme.

The background for this vision shows the sky with storm clouds, heavy seas, and land with cracks resulting from the earthquake. The city was divided into three parts, with figures falling from the weight of the hail.

The Harlot

Revelation 17:1-16

[1] One of the seven angels who had the seven bowls came and said to me, "Come, I will show you the punishment of the great prostitute, who sits on many waters. [2] With her the kings of the earth committed adultery and the inhabitants of the earth were intoxicated with the wine of her adulteries."

[3] Then the angel carried me away in the Spirit into a desert. There I saw a woman sitting on a scarlet beast that was covered with blasphemous names and had seven heads and ten horns.

[4] The woman was dressed in purple and scarlet, and was glittering with gold, precious stones and pearls. She had a golden cup in her hand, willed with abominable things and the filth of her adulteries. [5] This title was written on her forehead: MYSTERY BABYLON THE GREAT THE MOTHER OF PROSTITUTES AND OF THE ABOMINATIONS OF THE EARTH. [6] I saw that the woman was drunk with the blood of the saints, the blood of those who bore testimony to Jesus.

When I saw her, I was greatly astonished. [7] Then the angel said to me: "Why are you astonished? I will explain to you the mystery of the woman and of the beast she rides, which has the seven heads and ten horns. [8] The beast, which you saw, once was, now is not, and will come up out of the Abyss and go to his destruction. The inhabitants of the earth whose names have not been written in the book of life from the creation of the world will be astonished when they see the beast, because he once was, now is not, and yet will come.

[9] "This calls for a mind with wisdom. The seven heads are seven hills on which the woman sits. [10] They are also seven kings. Five have fallen, one is, the other has not yet come; but when he does come, he must remain for a little while. [11] The beast who once was, and now is not, is an eighth king. he belongs to the seven and is going to his destruction.

[12] "The ten horns you saw are ten kings who have not yet received a kingdom, but who for one hour will receive authority as kings along with the beast. [13] They have one purpose and will give their power and authority to the beast. [14] They will make war against the Lamb, but the Lamb will overcome them because he is Lord of lords and King of kings — and with him will be his called, chosen and faithful followers."

[15] Then the angel said to me, "The waters you saw, where the prostitute sits, are peoples, multitudes, nations and languages. [16] The beast and the ten horns you saw will hate the prostitute. They will bring her to ruin and leave her naked; they will eat her flesh and burn her with fire.

One of the seven angels appears to show John the judgment on the great harlot. The woman is sitting on a scarlet colored beast with seven heads and ten horns, and full of names of blasphemy. She is arrayed in purple and scarlet, and decked with gold and pearls and precious stones, with a golden cup (full of abominations) in her hand. She has a name, "Mystery, Babylon the Great, the Mother of Harlots and Abominations of the Earth," written on her forehead. She is drunk with the blood of the saints and the martyrs. The angel is shown in the bottom left foreground, explaining the meaning of the scene to John. The sea shows the "many waters".

The City of Sin

Revelation 17:9; 18:24

17:9
"This calls for a mind with wisdom. The seven heads are seven hills on which the woman sits."

18:24
"In her was found the blood of prophets and of the saints, and of all who have been killed on the earth"

Pictured here is the destruction of the city of sin. In the center fore-ground, is a city (located on seven mountains) burning, with the smoke ascending up toward heaven. The harlot is disrobed and burning. Around the city are seven kings, dressed in scarlet, signifying those who ruled. The ten horns represented ten more kings who would be over the nations. They are seen in an arc in the front. To the left, right, and middle back-ground can be seen the people mourning for the great and beautiful and rich city, where trade and commerce had come to naught. The waters are "all the peoples." After John was shown this, another angel, with great power, came down from heaven, saying, "Babylon the great is fallen, is fallen, and is become the habitation of devils, and the hold of every foul spirit, a cage of every unclean and hateful bird." This powerful and glorious angel is seen in the center back-ground, shedding his light on the earth from heaven. In the left background is seen "another voice" from heaven, asking God's people to come out of the wicked city, and not to partake of their sins. Her destruction is coming. Groups of peoples, cities, and nations that mourn are seen standing afar off. In the right center background is seen a mighty angel with a millstone, casting it into the sea, signifying the destruction of the city.

The Marriage of the Lamb

Revelation 19:1-10

[1] After this I heard what sounded like the roar of a great multitude in heaven shouting: "Hallelujah! Salvation and glory and power belong to our God, [2] for true and just are his judgments. He has condemned the great prostitute who corrupted the earth by her adulteries. He has avenged on her the blood of his servants."

[3] And again they shouted: "Hallelujah! The smoke from her goes up for ever and ever."

[4] The twenty-four elders and the four living creatures fell down and worshiped God, who was seated on the throne. And they cried: "Amen, Hallelujah!"

[5] Then a voice came from the throne, saying: "Praise our God, all you his servants, you who fear him, both small and great!"

[6] Then I heard what sounded like a great multitude, like the roar of rushing waters and like loud peals of thunder, shouting: "Hallelujah! For our Lord God Almighty reigns.
[7] Let us rejoice and be glad and give him glory! For the wedding of the Lamb has come, and his bride has made herself ready. [8] Fine linen, bright and clean, was given her to wear." (Fine linen stands for the righteous acts of the saints.)

[9] Then the angel said to me, "Write: 'Blessed are those who are invited to the wedding supper of the Lamb!' " And he added, "These are the true words of God."

[10] At this I fell at his feet to worship him. But he said to me, "Do not do it! I am a fellow servant with you and with your brothers who hold to the testimony of Jesus. Worship God! For the testimony of Jesus is the spirit of prophecy."

This scene portrays the great rejoicing in heaven resulting from the victory over the great harlot. In the top background of the picture is the worship scene with God on the throne and many worshippers singing praises and giving honor to Him. The occasion was the marriage of the Lamb. In the center middle ground is shown a marriage feast spread with the Bride, the Lamb's wife, clothed in white linen. A blessing is given to all who are called to the marriage supper. In the center foreground can be seen figures who have answered the invitation and are judged worthy to sit at the supper. A wonderful privilege for the faithful!

John again shows human weakness in a vain attempt to worship the angel, but is again rebuked, "Worship God."

Faithful And True

Revelation 19:11-16

[11] I saw heaven standing open and there before me was a white horse, whose rider is called Faithful and True. With justice he judges and makes war. [12] His eyes are like blazing fire, and on his head are many crowns. He has a name written on him that no one knows but he himself. [13] He is dressed in a robe dipped in blood, and his name is the Word of God. [14] The armies of heaven were following him, riding on white horses and dressed in fine linen, white and clean. [15] Out of his mouth comes a sharp sword with which to strike down the nations. "He will rule them with an iron scepter." He treads the winepress of the fury of the wrath of God Almighty. [16] On his robe and on his thigh he has this name written: KING OF KINGS AND LORD OF LORDS.

Watching the history of the church unfold, John saw heaven opened. He saw a white horse with a rider called "Faithful and True," who was to judge and to make war. He was followed by the armies in heaven. The picture shows the rider having eyes like flames of fire, many crowns, garments dipped in blood, the name "King of Kings, Lord of Lords" on his vesture (the Latin abbreviation INRI was used) and on his thigh. The description is similar to the first vision which John saw.

In this "all-out" crusade against evil, the weapon used was the sword coming from the mouth of the one riding the white horse. The armies of heaven, dressed in white linen, on white horses, followed. Victory is in store for all who follow Jesus Christ, and who use as their only weapon the sword of the Spirit, the Word of God.

Angel In The Sun

Revelation 19:17-21

[17] And I saw an angel standing in the sun, who cried in a loud voice to all the birds flying in midair, "Come, gather together for the great supper of God,
[18] so that you may eat the flesh of kings, generals, and mighty men, of horses and their riders, and the flesh of all people, free and slave, small and great."
[19] Then I saw the beast and the kings of the earth and their armies gathered together to make war against the rider of the horse and his army. [20] But the beast was captured, and with him the false prophet who had performed the miraculous signs on his behalf. With these signs he had deluded those who had received the mark of the beast and worshiped his image. The two of them were thrown alive into the fiery lake of burning sulfur. [21] The rest of them were killed with the sword that came out of the mouth of the rider on the horse, and all the birds gorged themselves on their flesh.

Preceding verses show that preparation was complete for a great battle. Jesus Christ and His cavalry were ready, having the mighty and powerful sword, the word of God, as their weapon. The armies of the kings of the earth, with the beast and false prophet, were gathered together in readiness for war. An angel stood in the sun and called for all the fowls that fly in the midst of heaven to come together for a great feast after the battle. The angel is pictured in a disk which represents the sun, and fowls are coming from all directions, gathering at the battleground. Two figures are shown in the center holding the beast and false prophet over their heads, casting them "alive into a lake of fire burning with brimstone." In the left background is pictured Christ and His cavalry of victors. This deceiving force was at an end. The faithful and true conquered!

Satan Bound

Revelation 20:1-6

[1] And I saw an angel coming down out of heaven, having the key to the Abyss and holding in his hand a great chain. [2] He seized the dragon, that ancient serpent, who is the devil, or Satan, and bound him for a thousand years. [3] He threw him into the Abyss, and locked and sealed it over him, to keep him from deceiving the nations anymore until the thousand years were ended. After that he must be set free for a short time.

[4] I saw thrones on which were seated those who had been given authority to judge. And I saw the souls of those who had been beheaded because of their testimony for Jesus and because of the word of God. They had not worshiped the beast or his image and had not received his mark on their foreheads or their hands. They came to life and reigned with Christ a thousand years. [5] (The rest of the dead did not come to life until the thousand years were ended.) This is the first resurrection. [6] Blessed and holy are those who have part in the first resurrection. The second death has no power over them, but they will be priests of God and of Christ and will reign with him for a thousand years.

John saw an angel come down from heaven, having a great chain and a key to the bottomless pit. Satan was bound for a thousand years. In the painting, the angel has caught, and chained, the dragon and is in the act of putting him in the bottomless pit. The key is in his hand, ready to lock it up. After this account, thrones and the ones who sat upon them were seen as judgment was given to them. They are shown in the picture on top of a cloud. Also shown are the souls of the martyrs for the witness of Jesus and the word of God. They are pictured holding their heads — beheaded. They lived and reigned with Christ.

Gog And Magog

Revelation 20:7-10

[7] When the thousand years are over, Satan will be released from his prison [8] and will go out to deceive the nations in the four corners of the earth — God and Magog — to gather them for battle. In number they are like the sand on the seashore. [9] They marched across the breadth of the earth and surrounded the camp of God's people, the city he loves. But fire came down from heaven and devoured them. [10] And the devil, who deceived them, was thrown into the lake of burning sulfur, where the beast and the false prophet had been thrown. They will be tormented day and night for ever and ever.

This scene begins with the thou-sand years end. Satan has his last fling, to deceive the nations in the four quarters of the earth — Gog and Magog. He gathers the numberless hosts together, and they surround the camp of the saints. But fire comes down from heaven and devours them. God's faithful and true are always victorious!

The grand climax is reached when Satan is cast into the lake of fire where the beast and the false prophet are — they shall all be tormented day and night forever and ever.

In the foreground are two figures to represent Gog and Magog, directing the great invasion from the north. Fire is seen coming down from heaven and falling on their armies. In the top background is the devil as he was cast into the lake of fire.

The Book Of Life

Revelation 20:11-15

[11] Then I saw a great white throne and him who was seated on it. Earth and sky fled from his presence, and there was no place for them. [12] And I saw the dead, great and small, standing before the throne, and books were opened. Another book was opened, which is the book of life. The dead were judged according to what they had done as recorded in the books. [13] The sea gave up the dead that were in it, and death and Hades gave up the dead that were in them, and each person was judged according to what he had done. [14] Then death and Hades were thrown into the lake of fire. The lake of fire is the second death. [15] If anyone's name was not found written in the book of life, he was thrown into the lake of fire.

This picture is the climax of the series. The judgment day has arrived, and before Him is gathered all the nations of all ages. The guilty are to be sentenced to everlasting punishment, while the righteous — those whose names are written in the Lamb's Book of Life — will be rewarded with an abundant entrance into heaven itself.

No one can adequately picture the face of God! Hence, this picture was painted from the perspective shown. The hands are shown holding a large scroll which is as clear as glass. The idea of the book in this painting is to show names, the letters can almost — but not quite — be read! Between the arms, and behind in the center fore-ground, are figures which represent the dead, both small and great. They are depicted as they departed this life — of every age, in dress both modern and ancient, of every race and color. Part of the great white throne and part of the feet can be seen from this perspective. Also is shown the other books opened in front of the figures. The clouds painted in the heavens depict the glory of God. The extreme right foreground are figures rising from the sea as it gave up its dead. To the left foreground, hell is giving up its dead — with skeletons and graves being cast into the lake of fire. Truly, "the last enemy to be destroyed is death," and John here records it as a blessing and a warning to all generations.

The New Heaven And The New Earth

Revelation 21:1-8

[1] Then I saw a new heaven and a new earth, for the first heaven and the first earth had passed away, and there was no longer any sea. [2] I saw the Holy City, the new Jerusalem, coming down out of heaven from God, prepared as a bride beautifully dressed for her husband. [3] And I heard a loud voice from the throne saying, "Now the dwelling of God is with men, and he will live with them. They will be his people, and God himself will be with them and be their God. [4] He will wipe every tear from their eyes. There will be no more death or mourning or crying or pain, for the old order of things has passed away."

[5] He who was seated on the throne said, "I am making everything new!" Then he said, "Write this down, for these words are trustworthy and true."

[6] He said to me: "It is done. I am the Alpha and the Omega, the Beginning and the End. To him who is thirsty I will give to drink without cost from the spring of the water of life. [7] He who overcomes will inherit all this, and I will be his God and he will be my son. [8] But the cowardly, the unbelieving, the vile, the murderers, the sexually immoral, those who practice magic arts, the idolaters and all liars — their place will be in the fiery lake of burning sulfur. This is the second death."

Every soul should be moved to be faithful and true until death when he reads this word picture of the scene of the Holy City, the New Jerusalem, coming down from God out of heaven, prepared as a bride adorned for her husband — when he contemplates a place where there is no death, no sorrow, no crying, no pain, none of the former things, and where God shall wipe away all tears from their eyes. Such is God's promise to the faithful. "I will be his God, and he shall be my Son."

The painting is composed from many passages concerning the New Jerusalem — from the prophets to the end of Revelation. It shows a city in gold, as clear as glass, with the glory of God pictured with a cloud formation to resemble a bridal veil adorning the city coming down from heaven. In the foreground can be seen rocks which show the Isle of Patmos. John is shown watching this magnificent scene, with rays of light coming down from the city.

The City Foursquare

Revelation 21:9-27

[9] One of the seven angels who had the seven bowls full of the seven last plagues came and said to me, "Come, I will show you the bride, the wife of the Lamb." [10] And he carried me away in the Spirit to a mountain great and high, and showed me the Holy City, Jerusalem, coming down out of heaven from God. [11] It shone with the glory of God, and its brilliance was like that of a very precious jewel, like a jasper, clear as crystal. [12] It had a great, high wall with twelve gates, and with twelve angels at the gates. On the gates were written the names of the twelve tribes of Israel. [13] There were three gates on the east, three on the north, three on the south and three on the west. [14] The wall of the city had twelve foundations, and on them were the names of the *twelve apostles of the Lamb.*

[15] The angel who talked with me had a measuring rod of gold to measure the city, its gates and its walls. [16] The city was laid out like a square, as long as it was wide. He measured the city with the rod and found it to be 12,000 stadia in length, and as wide and high as it is long. [17] He measured its wall and it was 144 cubits thick, by man's measurement, which the angel was using. [18] The wall was made of jasper, and the city of pure gold, as pure as glass. [19] The foundations of the city walls were decorated with every kind of precious stone. The first foundation was jasper, the second sapphire, the third chalcedony, the fourth emerald, [20] the fifth sardonyx, the sixth carnelian, the seventh chrysolite, the eighth beryl, the ninth topaz, the tenth chrysoprase, the eleventh jacinth, and the twelfth amethyst.

[21] The twelve gates were twelve pearls, each gate made of a single pearl. The great street of the city was of pure gold, like transparent glass.

[22] I did not see a temple in the city, because the Lord God Almighty and the Lamb are its temple. [23] The city does not need the sun or the moon to shine on it, for the glory of God gives it light, and the Lamb is its lamp. [24] The nations will walk by its light, and the kings of the earth will bring their splendor into it. [25] On no day will its gates ever be shut, for there will be no night there. [26] The glory and honor of the nations will be brought into it. [27] Nothing impure will ever enter it, nor will anyone who does what is shameful or deceitful, but only those whose names are written in the Lamb's book of life.

Descriptions of beauty, grandeur, and splendor reach a climax with the account of John's vision of the city foursquare. The city had the glory of God — a Jasper light, a massive wall with twelve gates of pearl, each with an angel near by. An angel measured the city with a golden reed — and the length, breadth, and height were the same. There were twelve foundations, each containing the name of an apostle. The painting is composed of colors to be found in the foundation stones. Attempting to imagine these colors with the sparkle of a diamond, clear as crystal, in such a breath-taking scene, is truly an uplift of the soul.

The River Of Life

Revelation 22:1-5

[1] Then the angel showed me the river of the water of life, as clear as crystal, flowing from the throne of God and of the Lamb [2] down the middle of the great street of the city. On each side of the river stood the tree of life, bearing twelve crops of fruit, yielding its fruit every month. And the leaves of the tree are for the healing of the nations. [3] No longer will there be any curse. The throne of God and of the Lamb will be in the city, and his servants will serve him. [4] They will see his face, and his name will be on their foreheads. [5] There will be no more night. They will not need the light of a lamp or the light of the sun, for the Lord God will give them light. And they will reign for ever and ever.

In great splendor, John was shown the river of the water of life, crystal clear, coming from the throne of God and the Lamb. The painting is a com-position of the imagination rendered from the word picture. The back-ground is reflected light behind the throne, resembling the Aurora Borealis. The street was painted shades of yellow to portray gold, with water running in the middle. The tree of Life is pictured on either side of the river with its twelve different fruits, each painted a different color. Clouds were used to symbolize the glory of God's presence.